QED ESSENTIALS

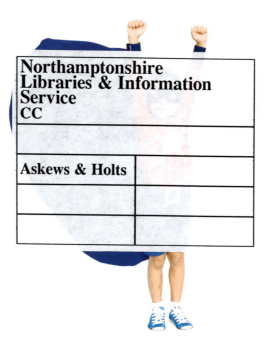

Quarto is the authority on a wide range of topics.

Quarto educates, entertains and enriches the lives of our readers—enthusiasts and lovers of hands-on living.

www.quartoknows.com

Author: Simon Mugford
Series Editor: Joyce Bentley
Editor: Sasha Morton
Consultant: Helen Marron
Designer: Elaine Wilkinson

First published in 2019 by QED Publishing,
an imprint of The Quarto Group.
The Old Brewery, 6 Blundell Street,
London N7 9BH, United Kingdom.
T (0)20 7700 6700 F (0)20 7700 8066
www.QuartoKnows.com

MIX
Paper from
responsible sources
FSC® C001701

Manufactured in Shenzhen, China PP072019

9 8 7 6 5 4 3 2 1

A catalogue record for this book is available from the British Library.

ISBN: 978-0-7112-4426-9

Photo Acknowledgments
Shutterstock: front cover StockImageFactory.com; back cover and imprint page Rawpixel.com; title page and p8-9 Rawpixel.com; p3 and 6 Rob Hainer; p4-5 Sergey Novikov; p7 and 20 Africa Studio; p10-11 and 20 Rawpixel.com; p12 StockImageFactory.com; p12-13 and 20 vectorfusionart; p14 and 20 Tomsickova Tatyana; p15t and 20 Kiselev Andrey Valerich; p15b Serenko Natalia; p16-17 and 22 Maya Kruchanokova; p18l Julia Kuznetsova; p18r Sergey Sukhorukov; p19b and 20 vectorfusionart; p21 Anastasia Shilova

Dressing Up

Dressing up is lots of fun!

I am
a pirate.

4

We can dress up in masks.

We can dress up in hats and wigs.

We can dress up like grown-ups.

He can dress up as a superhero.

Look at my cape!

She can dress up to fly a plane.

We can dress up to go in a rocket.

Zoom!

He can dress up like a wizard.

She can dress up like an elf.

They can dress up as animals.

We can all dress up.

pirate

dragon

18

superhero

What will you dress up as?

queen

19

Your Turn

Match it!

Follow the line from each picture
to read the word.

wizard

queen

rocket

superhero

wig

Clap it!

Say the 'Match it!' words. Clap and count the syllables.

Sound it!

Sound out each of these words.

d r e ss   w i ng s   w oo f   c l u ck

Say it!

Read and say these words.

he   we   she   all   they

Spot it!

(1) Look at page 11. Which word has a short **oo** sound?

(2) Look at page 15. Which word begins with a **w** sound?

Finish it!

Look back and find which word is missing.

(1) Look at page 7. We can dress up in _____ and wigs.

(2) Look at page 12. She can dress up to fly a _____ .

Count it!

(1) Look at pages 4-5. How many words have two letters?

(2) Look at page 13. Which word has five letters?

Answers: **Spot it!** 1 Look 2 wizard **Finish it!** 1 hats 2 plane **Count it!** 1 four (up, is, of, am) 2 wings

Sort it!

Sort the letters to spell a word.
Can you find the word in the book?

1 | e | r | o | t | ck

2 | n | a | g | r | o | d

3 | k | s | m | a

4 | m | oo | z

Do it!

Draw yourself in one of the
dressing up costumes from the book.
Describe your costume to a friend.

Notes for Parents and Teachers

Children naturally practise their literacy skills as they discover the world around them. The topics in the **QED Essentials** series help children use these developing skills and broaden their knowledge and vocabulary. Once they have finished reading the text, encourage your child to demonstrate their understanding by having a go at the activities on pages 20–23.

Reading Tips

• Sit next to your child and let them turn the pages themselves.

• Look through the book before you start reading together. Discuss what you can see on the cover first.

• Encourage your child to use a finger to track the text as they read.

• Keep reading and talking sessions short and at a time that works for both of you. Try to make it a relaxing moment to share with your child.

• Prompt your child to use the picture clues to support their reading when they come across unfamiliar words.

• Give lots of praise as your child reads and return to the book as often as you can. Re-reading leads to greater confidence and fluency.

• Remind your child to use their letter sound knowledge to work out new words.

• Use the 'Your Turn' pages to practise reading new words and to encourage your child to talk about the text.

We can dress up to go in a rocket.

Zoom!

He can dress up like a wizard.

She can dress up like an elf.

Colourful photographs open up further discussion points

Wide range of vocabulary to explore in context

Short, decodable sentences repeat topic words and commonly used words